by Iain Gray

Lang**Syne**

PUBLISHING

WRITING *to* REMEMBER

79 Main Street, Newtongrange,
Midlothian EH22 4NA
Tel: 0131 344 0414   Fax: 0845 075 6085
E-mail: info@lang-syne.co.uk
www.langsyneshop.co.uk

Design by Dorothy Meikle
Printed by Printwell Ltd
© Lang Syne Publishers Ltd 2016

ISBN 978-1-85217-525-2

Clarke

MOTTO:
Seize the day.

CREST:
A lark rising.

NAME variations include:
Clark
Clerke

Chapter one:

The origins of popular surnames

by George Forbes and Iain Gray

If you don't know where you came from, you won't know where you're going is a frequently quoted observation and one that has a particular resonance today when there has been a marked upsurge in interest in genealogy, with increasing numbers of people curious to trace their family roots.

Main sources for genealogical research include census returns and official records of births, marriages and deaths – and the key to unlocking the detail they contain is obviously a family surname, one that has been 'inherited' and passed from generation to generation.

No matter our station in life, we all have a surname – but it was not until about the middle of the fourteenth century that the practice of being identified by a particular surname became commonly established throughout the British Isles.

Previous to this, it was normal for a person to be identified through the use of only a forename.

But as population gradually increased and there were many more people with the same forename, surnames were adopted to distinguish one person, or community, from another.

Many common English surnames are patronymic in origin, meaning they stem from the forename of one's father – with 'Johnson,' for example, indicating 'son of John.'

It was the Normans, in the wake of their eleventh century conquest of Anglo-Saxon England, a pivotal moment in the nation's history, who first brought surnames into usage – although it was a gradual process.

For the Normans, these were names initially based on the title of their estates, local villages and chateaux in France to distinguish and identify these landholdings.

Such grand descriptions also helped enhance the prestige of these warlords and generally glorify their lofty positions high above the humble serfs slaving away below in the pecking order who had only single names, often with Biblical connotations as in Pierre and Jacques.

The only descriptive distinctions among the peasantry concerned their occupations, like 'Pierre the swineherd' or 'Jacques the ferryman.'

Roots of surnames that came into usage in England not only included Norman-French, but also Old French, Old Norse, Old English, Middle English, German, Latin, Greek, Hebrew and the Gaelic languages of the Celts.

The Normans themselves were originally Vikings, or 'Northmen', who raided, colonised and eventually settled down around the French coastline.

The had sailed up the Seine in their longboats in 900AD under their ferocious leader Rollo and ruled the roost in north eastern France before sailing over to conquer England in 1066 under Duke William of Normandy – better known to posterity as William the Conqueror, or King William I of England.

Granted lands in the newly-conquered England, some of their descendants later acquired territories in Wales, Scotland and Ireland – taking not only their own surnames, but also the practice of adopting a surname, with them.

But it was in England where Norman rule and custom first impacted, particularly in relation to the adoption of surnames.

This is reflected in the famous *Domesday Book*, a massive survey of much of England and Wales, ordered by William I, to determine who owned what, what it was worth and therefore how much they were liable to pay in taxes to the voracious Royal Exchequer.

Completed in 1086 and now held in the National Archives in Kew, London, 'Domesday' was an Old English word meaning 'Day of Judgement.'

This was because, in the words of one contemporary chronicler, "its decisions, like those of the Last Judgement, are unalterable."

It had been a requirement of all those English landholders – from the richest to the poorest – that they identify themselves for the purposes of the survey and for future reference by means of a surname.

This is why the *Domesday Book*, although written in Latin as was the practice for several centuries with both civic and ecclesiastical records, is an invaluable source for the early appearance of a wide range of English surnames.

Several of these names were coined in connection with occupations.

These include Baker and Smith, while Cooks, Chamberlains, Constables and Porters were to be found carrying out duties in large medieval households.

The church's influence can be found in names such as Bishop, Friar and Monk while the popular name of Bennett derives from the late fifth to mid-sixth century Saint Benedict, founder of the Benedictine order of monks.

The early medical profession is represented by Barber, while businessmen produced names that include Merchant and Sellers.

Down at the village watermill, the names that cropped up included Millar/Miller, Walker and Fuller, while other self-explanatory trades included Cooper, Tailor, Mason and Wright.

Even the scenery was utilised as in Moor, Hill, Wood and Forrest – while the hunt and the chase supplied names that include Hunter, Falconer, Fowler and Fox.

Colours are also a source of popular surnames, as in Black, Brown, Gray/Grey, Green and White, and would have denoted the colour of the clothing the person habitually wore or, apart from the obvious exception of 'Green', one's hair colouring or even complexion.

The surname Red developed into Reid, while

Blue was rare and no-one wanted to be associated with yellow.

Rather self-important individuals took surnames that include Goodman and Wiseman, while physical attributes crept into surnames such as Small and Little.

Many families proudly boast the heraldic device known as a Coat of Arms, as featured on our front cover.

The central motif of the Coat of Arms would originally have been what was borne on the shield of a warrior to distinguish himself from others on the battlefield.

Not featured on the Coat of Arms, but high-lighted on page three, is the family motto and related crest – with the latter frequently different from the central motif.

Adding further variety to the rich cultural heritage that is represented by surnames is the appearance in recent times in lists of the 100 most common names found in England of ones that include Khan, Patel and Singh – names that have proud roots in the vast sub-continent of India.

Echoes of a far distant past can still be found in our surnames and they can be borne with pride in commemoration of our forebears.

Chapter two:

Persecution and civil war

Originally an occupational designation that developed into a surname, 'Clarke' is ranked 26th in some lists of the 100 most common surnames found in England today, while its spelling variant of 'Clark' is ranked 28th.

Derived from the Latin *clericus*, it denoted someone who in the Middle Ages was literate or scholarly enough to be employed in a religious order as a scribe or as a secretary in a royal household or in the manor house of a lord.

Its Gaelic form is *cleireach*, which gave rise to the Irish names 'Cleary' and 'MacCleary', while in Scotland, where 'Clark' is the most common form found today, bearers of the name are recognised as a sept, or sub-branch, of the proud Clan Macpherson.

Despite its Gaelic forms, the name is of Anglo-Saxon roots, and flowing through the veins of many people of English birth today such as the Clarkes and the Clarks is the blood of those Germanic tribes who invaded and settled in the south and east of the island of Britain from about the early fifth century.

Known as the Anglo-Saxons, they were composed of the Jutes, from the area of the Jutland Peninsula in modern Denmark, the Saxons from Lower Saxony, in modern Germany and the Angles from the Angeln area of Germany.

It was the Angles who gave the name 'Engla land', or 'Aengla land' – better known as 'England', and they held sway from approximately 550 until the Norman Conquest of 1066, with the main kingdoms those of Sussex, Wessex, Northumbria, Mercia, Kent, East Anglia and Essex.

In England, the name is first found in the ancient Anglo-Saxon kingdom of Kent – but its bearers came to be found all over the British Isles and feature prominently in the historical record.

One particularly unfortunate bearer was Elizabeth Clarke, the first woman to be persecuted by the notorious 'Witchfinder General' Matthew Hopkins.

The title of 'Witchfinder General' was one that Hopkins bestowed upon himself and, during a reign of terror that lasted from 1645 to 1647, he and his colleague John Stearne are believed to have been responsible for the deaths of 300 women who had been maliciously accused of witchcraft.

Their witch-hunts took place mainly in Norfolk, Suffolk and Essex – and it was in the latter eastern English county that Elizabeth Clarke, a frail 80-year-old woman with only one leg, came to their attention in 1645 after being accused of witchcraft by a local tailor, John Rivet.

Hopkins, who had penned his own book on witchcraft, *The Discovery of Witches*, used a number of techniques to extract so-called confessions from his helpless and bewildered victims.

Among these techniques was sleep deprivation, and it was after being subjected to such an ordeal over a lengthy period that Elizabeth Clarke finally 'confessed.'

She was duly hung from a gibbet, the first of the fanatical Witchfinder General's many victims.

In the same century, John Clark was the Parliamentary soldier and politician who held a number of powerful posts.

The monarch Charles I had incurred the wrath of Parliament by his insistence on the 'divine right' of monarchs, and added to this was Parliament's fear of Catholic 'subversion' against the state and the king's stubborn refusal to grant demands for religious and constitutional concessions.

Matters came to a head with the outbreak of the English Civil War in 1642, with Parliamentary forces, known as the New Model Army and commanded by Oliver Cromwell and Sir Thomas Fairfax, arrayed against the Royalist army of the king.

In what became an increasingly bloody and complex conflict, spreading to Scotland and Ireland and with rapidly shifting loyalties on both sides, the 49-year-old king was eventually captured and executed in January of 1649 on the orders of Parliament.

A colonel in the New Model Army, John Clark benefited directly from the 1649 Cromwellian invasion of Ireland.

It had been in 1641 that insurrection exploded on the island, with at least 2,000 Protestant settlers massacred at the hands of Catholic landowners and their native Irish peasantry, while thousands more were stripped of their belongings and driven from their lands.

Terrible as the atrocities were against the Protestant settlers, subsequent accounts became greatly exaggerated and served to fuel a burning desire on the part of Protestants for revenge against the rebels.

The Civil War had intervened to prevent

immediate action being taken, but following the execution of Charles I and the subsequent consolidation of Cromwell's power, the time was ripe for revenge.

The self-styled Lord Protector descended on Ireland at the head of a 20,000-strong army that landed at Ringford, near Dublin, in August of 1649 – and in its ranks was Colonel John Clark.

Cromwell had three main aims: to quash all forms of rebellion, to 'remove' all Catholic landowners who had taken part in the rebellion and to convert the Native Irish to the Protestant faith.

His forces soon held Ireland in a grip of iron and soldiers who had fought for him were granted lands confiscated from those deemed to have been rebels.

As reward for his services, Clark was appointed Commissioner of Irish Affairs and, in 1654, Governor of Londonderry.

Following the death of Cromwell in 1658, it was Clark who signed the order proclaiming his son, Richard Cromwell, as the 'Protector.'

But Clark's downfall came in the wake of the Restoration of Charles II in 1660, when he was imprisoned for treason.

He is known to have petitioned the king for his release, but his subsequent fate is not known.

The brothers Samuel and John Clarke appear in the historical record through more peaceful endeavours.

Born in Norwich in 1675, the son of a textile manufacturer, Samuel Clarke was the Anglican clergyman and philosopher who served as chaplain to John Moore, Bishop of Norwich.

He died in 1729, while his brother John, born in 1682, was the natural philosopher and cleric who served from 1728 until his death in 1757 as Dean of Salisbury.

His noted works include his two-volume *An Enquiry into the Cause and Origin of Evil*, published in 1720.

Physician to Queen Victoria and Albert, the Prince Consort, James Clark was the eminent Scottish surgeon born in 1788 in Cullen, Banffshire.

Educated at Aberdeen University, where he obtained an arts degree, he later studied medicine at Edinburgh University, becoming a member of the Royal College of Surgeons.

Serving for a time as a surgeon with the Royal Navy, he later travelled throughout Europe carrying out pioneering research into how climatic changes affect what was then the killer disease of tuberculosis.

Settling in Rome in 1819, one of his patients was the English poet John Keats.

Returning to Britain, he was appointed Queen Victoria's Physician-in-Ordinary in 1837 and, three years later, physician to Prince Albert.

Created a Baronet in the Peerage of the United Kingdom and the author of an important 1835 work on the causes, nature, prevention and treatment of tuberculosis, he died in 1870.

Chapter three:

PR and politics

Bearers of the Clarke and Clark names also feature in the historical record of nations far removed from their original homeland of the British Isles.

One colourful such character was Richard Clarke who, born in Yorkshire in 1845 and later immigrating to the United States, became famous as a frontiersman and Pony Express rider.

The inspiration for the fictional character *Deadwood Dick*, it was as a Pony Express rider that he frequently had to defend himself with rifle and gun in hand against the Native American Sioux.

He lived in Deadwood, South Dakota, and it was here that he died in 1930 – having already provided the colourful inspiration for Edward Lytton Wheeler's best-selling *Deadwood Dick* series of 'dime' novels, published between 1877 and 1897.

Not only a war correspondent but also a propaganda expert and an early pioneer of public relations, more popularly known as PR, Thomas Clarke was born in 1879 in Altrincham, near Manchester.

Rebelling against his widowed mother's plan

for him to enter the banking profession because he was more interested in a career in music, he travelled throughout Europe earning a living by playing the piano in a range of venues that included cinemas.

Switching careers, before the outbreak of the First World War in 1914 he joined the staff of the *Sunday Times*, later moving to the *Daily Mail* – and it was this newspaper that despatched him to the Western Front as a war correspondent.

Appointed director of special intelligence at the Ministry of Reconstruction at the end of the conflict, he was later appointed head of the British Government's propaganda unit, the Public Information Department.

Leaving Government service in the early 1920s, he set up Editorial Services, Britain's first PR agency.

In 1924, he published his famous *Little White Book*, which introduced the first code of ethics for PR.

Long before the controversies that today surround the relationship between PR companies, newspapers and government, he stated:

All anonymity or disguise on the part of the
PR operator must go. No payment must be
accepted from newspapers. No canvassing for

> *accounts. No fraudulent stunts likely to*
> *deceive the public, or editors.*

Clarke also wrote a number of speeches for George V, with the monarch at one time telling him: "Clarke, I like the speeches you write for me. You don't make me sound too bloody pompous."

Honoured with a knighthood, Clarke, who died in 1947, is also credited with having successfully campaigned for a ban in Britain on harmful colouring matter and adulterants in preserved foods and for the use of pasteurised milk for babies.

This was while he acted as PR representative in Britain for America's Heinz organisation.

Responsible for popularising the history of art, Kenneth Mackenzie Clark, better known as Kenneth Clark, was the eminent British author and television broadcaster born in 1903 in London.

Of Scottish roots through his father and educated at Trinity College, Oxford, where he studied the history of art, he is best known for having been the writer, producer and presenter of the internationally acclaimed 1969 BBC Television series *Civilisation*.

Appointed director of the National Gallery at the age of 30, the youngest person to date to have held the post, and the recipient of honours and awards that included a knighthood, he died in 1983.

Also one of the founders in 1954 of Britain's Independent Television Authority (ITA) and serving as its first chairman before moving three years later to the BBC, he was the father of the Conservative Party politician and military historian Alan Clark.

Serving in ministerial posts during the tenure of Prime Minister Margaret Thatcher that included defence and known for his acerbic wit and rakish lifestyle, he is best remembered for his three-volume *Diaries* (1972-1999).

As a military historian, he wrote the controversial *The Donkeys, A History of the British Expeditionary Force in 1915*, published in 1961 and believed to have inspired the musical satire *Oh, What a Lovely War!*

Also the author of other works that include his 1963 *The Fall of Crete*, he died in 1999.

In contemporary British politics, Kenneth Harry Clarke, is the Conservative party politician better known as Ken Clarke.

Born in 1940 near Nottingham, he held a number of senior Government posts from 1979 to 1997 that include Home Secretary and Chancellor of the Exchequer – serving in the Cabinets of Prime Minister Margaret Thatcher and then John Major.

Member of Parliament (MP) for Rushcliffe, he was appointed by Conservative Prime Minister David Cameron in 2010 as Lord Chancellor and Secretary of State for Justice.

In British Labour Party politics, Charles Clarke, born in London in 1951, is the former Government minister and MP for Norwich South from 1997 to 2010 who held posts that include, from 2004 to 2006, Home Secretary.

Also in British Labour Party politics, Tom Clarke is the Scottish MP born in 1941 in Coatbridge, Lanarkshire.

Representing Coatbridge, Chryston and Bellshill, he is also a keen supporter of British film-making and has served in a number of film-related posts that include deputy director of the Scottish Film Council.

Born in 1950, Helen Clark served three consecutive terms from 1999 to 2008 as the 37th Prime Minister of New Zealand, the first woman to hold the post.

First elected to Parliament in 1981 as a member of the New Zealand Labour Party, she retired from politics in 2009 and took up the post of administrator of the United Nations Development Programme (UNDP).

In Canadian politics, Charles Joseph Clark, better known as Joe Clark, served as leader of the former Progressive Conservative Party as 16th Prime Minister of Canada from June of 1979 to March of 1980.

Born in 1939 in High River, Alberta, he is the youngest person to date to have held the post; he retired from politics in 2004.

In American politics, Richard Clarke served in the administrations of three Presidents – Bill Clinton, George H.W. Bush and George W. Bush – as an advisor on counter-terrorism.

He caused controversy in 2004 when his memoirs about his service in government, *Against All Enemies* and his testimony before the 9/11 Commission were highly critical of the George W. Bush administration's stance towards counter-terrorism before the 9/11 attacks on America and of the decision to go to war with Iraq.

Born in 1950 in Dorchester, Massachusetts, he is now retired from government service.

Chapter four:

On the world stage

Bearers of the Clarke name and its popular spelling variant of Clark have gained international recognition through a colourful range of pursuits.

Best known for her role of Nina Myers in the popular American television drama series *24*, **Sarah Clarke** is the American actress born in 1972 in St Louis, Missouri.

Also known as Sarah Berkeley following her marriage to fellow *24* actor Xander Berkeley, her big screen credits includes the 2008 *Twilight*.

Born in 1969 in Dana Point, California, **Melinda Clarke**, also known as Mindy Clarke, is the actress best known for her role of Faith Taylor in the television drama *Days of Our Lives*, while other television credits include *The O.C.* and *Nikita*.

Behind the camera lens, **Jim Clark** is the British film director and editor who received an Academy Award and a BAFTA Award for his editing of the 1984 *The Killing Fields*.

Born in 1931 in Boston, Lancashire and also the recipient of a BAFTA Award for editing the 1986 film *The Mission*, he received the American Cinema Career Achievement Award in 2005.

Killed along with his 22-year-old son in a car accident in 2007, **Bob Clark** was the American actor, director, screenwriter and producer born in New Orleans in 1939.

Working mainly in the United States, where he directed and co-wrote the script for the 1983 *A Christmas Story*, from 1973 to 1983 he was responsible for a number of acclaimed Canadian films.

These include the 1974 *Black Christmas*, the 1980 *Decree* and, from 1982, *Porky's*.

Born in 1935 in Wallasey, Cheshire, **Alan Clarke** was the British television and film director, writer and producer who specialised in often controversial works of social realism.

His 1977 play *Scum*, dealing with borstals – as youth prisons were once known in the United Kingdom – was banned by the BBC but released by Clarke two years later as a feature film of the same name.

Other screen credits include the 1987 *Rita, Sue and Bob Too* and the 1989 *The Firm*, starring Gary Oldman.

Also the director of the 1982 British television

drama *Made in Britain*, based on a screenplay by David Leland, he died in 1990.

Also on British television screens, **Roy Clarke** is the former teacher, policeman and soldier best known as the creator of the BBC comedy series *Last of the Summer Wine*.

Born in 1930 in Austerfield, Yorkshire and also the writer of other popular comedy series that include *Open All Hours* and *Keeping up Appearances*, his many awards include the Lifetime Achievement Award at the 2010 British Comedy Awards.

From film and television to the world of the written word, **Arthur C. Clarke** was the renowned British science fiction writer, inventor and futurist born in 1917 in Minehead, Somerset.

Known, along with Isaac Asimov and Robert A. Heinlein as having been one of the "Big Three" of science fiction, it was while serving in the Royal Air Force as a radar technician and instructor that in 1945 he proposed a satellite communication system.

A concept far ahead of its time, it was after such a system finally did come into operation that in 1963 he was awarded the prestigious Franklin Institute Gold Medal.

Serving as chairman of the British

Interplanetary Society from 1947 to 1950 and then again in 1953, he settled in Sri Lanka in 1956.

It was here that he died in 2008, the recipient of many honours that included a knighthood and the author of best-selling works that include his 1951 *The Sands of Mars* and, from 1968, his famous *2001: A Space Odyssey*, also successfully adapted for a film of the same name.

Born in 1959 in Nottingham, **Susanna Clarke** is the award-winning British author best known for her first novel, the 2004 *Jonathan Strange and Mr Norrell*.

The novel was the winner of a number of awards that include a World Fantasy Award for Best Novel, while her other works include the 2006 *The Ladies of Grace Adieu and other stories*.

A co-founder in 1944 of Dublin's Lyric Theatre Company, **Austin Clarke** was the influential Irish poet, playwright and novelist whose works include his 1955 poetry collection *Ancient Lights*.

Born in 1896 and also for a time the presenter of a weekly poetry programme on Irish radio, he died in 1974.

In contemporary times, **Gillian Clarke** is the poet, playwright and translator from the Welsh language born in Cardiff in 1937.

Appointed National Poet of Wales in 2008 and a recipient two years later of the Queen's Gold Medal for Poetry, her works include the 1971 *Snow on the Mountain* and, from 2009, *A Recipe for Water*.

In a much different poetic genre, **John Cooper Clarke**, born in 1949 in Salford, Lancashire is the English performance poet who during the late 1970's period of punk rock gained fame as a 'punk poet.'

His albums of verse include the 1978 *Disguise in Love* and, from 1982, *Zip Style Method*.

Bearers of the Clarke and Clark names have also excelled in the highly competitive world of sport – not least the famed Scottish motor racing champion **Jim Clark**.

Born into a farming family at Kilmany, Fife, in 1936 and moving at the age of six to Edington Mains farm in Duns, Berwickshire, as a Formula One racing driver he won the World Championship in 1963 and 1965 – the same year in which he also won the Indianapolis 500.

Killed in a Formula Two racing accident at Hockenheim, Germany in April of 1968, at the time of his death he had won 25 more Grand Prix races than any other driver.

Inducted in to the International Motorsports

Hall of Fame in 1990, his many other posthumous honours include an inaugural induction in 2002 to the Scottish Sports Hall of Fame.

From motor racing to the fields of European football, **Allan Clarke** is the former striker who won 19 caps playing for England between 1970 and 1975.

Born in 1946 in Willenhall, West Midlands and nicknamed "Sniffer", he played for teams that include Walsall, Leicester City and Leeds United, while he has also managed clubs that include Barnsley, Leeds United and Lincoln City.

From football to golf, **Darren Clarke**, awarded an OBE in 2012 for his services to golf, is the Northern Irish golfer who has won major tournaments that include the European Tour, the Professional Golfers Association (PGA) Tour and the Japan Golf Tour. Born in 1968 in Dungannon, Co. Tyrone, at the time of writing he has played in five Ryder Cup teams, while one of his most notable wins was the 2011 Open Championship at Royal St George's, in Sandwich, Kent.

In the boxing ring, **Chris Clarke** is the Canadian retired boxer, born in 1956 in Halifax, Nova Scotia, who won the gold medal in the lightweight division at the 1975 Pan American Games.

In the rough and tumble that is the game of rugby union, **Don Clarke**, nicknamed "The Boot" because of his goal-kicking ability, is the New Zealand former fullback who played for his country between 1956 and 1964; born in 1933 in Pihama, he died in 2002.

In the Canadian national sport of ice hockey, **Bobby Clarke** is the former centre who, between 1969 and 1984, played in the National Hockey league (NHL) for the Philadelphia Flyers.

During his career he helped the Philadelphia Flyers to win two prestigious Stanley Cups, while he later became an executive with the team.

Captain of Team Canada when it won the gold medal at the 1976 Canada Cup, his honours include appointment as an Officer of the Order of Canada and induction into the Hockey Hall of Fame.

From sport to music, **Allen Clarke** is the British retired singer who, along with Graham Nash, was one of the founders in 1963 of the British pop band the Hollies.

Born in 1942 in Salford, Lancashire, he enjoyed best-selling hits with the Hollies that include *Bus Stop*, *I'm Alive* and *He Ain't Heavy … He's My Brother*.

Born in 1957 in St Helens, Lancashire, **Peter Clarke** is the English drummer best known as having played from 1979 to 1996 with Siouxsie and the Banshees.

Across the Atlantic from Britain, Gilbert Clarke, better known as **Gibby Clarke**, is an American rock guitarist and record producer.

Born in 1962 in Cleveland, Ohio, he was rhythm guitarist for a time with Guns N' Roses, while he is also one of the founders of the band Rock Star Supernova.

Back on British shores, **Dave Clark**, born in 1942 in Tottenham, North London is the musician, songwriter and record producer who was the leader and drummer of the 1960s group The Dave Clark Five.

Inducted into the Rock and Roll Hall of Fame in 2008, the band enjoyed a number of international hits that include *Glad All Over*.

Ranked 11th on *Classic Rock* magazine's list of "100 Wildest Guitar Heroes", **Steve Clark**, born in Sheffield in 1960, was co-lead guitarist with the British heavy rock band Def Leppard from 1978 until his death in 1991.

Born in Coventry in 1941, **Tony Clarke** was

the English guitarist and record producer who, from 1966 to 1979, produced best-selling albums for the Moody Blues. Also the producer of albums for other artists who include Rick Wakeman and Clannad, he died in 2010.

Bearers of the proud name of Clarke have also stamped their mark on the disciplines of science and engineering.

Known as the "Father of Geochemistry", Frank Wigglesworth Clarke, better known as **F.W. Clarke**, was the American scientist and chemist credited with having determined the composition of the Earth's crust.

Born in Boston in 1847, he held a number of posts that included, from 1883 until six years before his death in 1931, Chief Chemist of the U.S. Geological Survey.

The mineral Clarkeite is named for him, as is the F.W. Clarke Award of the Geochemical Society.

Responsible for what is hailed as one of the major advances in preventative medicine in the second half of the twentieth century, **Sir Cyril Clarke** was the British physician and geneticist born in 1907 in Leicester.

The medical breakthrough for which he was

responsible was the development of a technique for the prevention of Rh disease in the new-born.

President of the Royal College of Physicians from 1972 to 1977, he died in 2000.

One particularly pioneering bearer of the Clarke name was **Edith Clarke**, the first woman to be employed as an electrical engineer in the United States and the nation's first female professor of the discipline.

Born in 1883, she graduated from Vassar College, Poughkeepsie, New York, in 1908 after studying mathematics and astronomy. Teaching mathematics for a time, she obtained a degree in electrical engineering from the Massachusetts Institute of Technology (MIT) in 1918.

But it was not until 1922 that she was hired by General Electric as an electrical engineer – having previously invented what is known as the Clarke Calculator, used to solve complex electrical equations.

Appointed a professor in the electrical engineering department at the University of Texas, Austin, in 1947 – the first woman to hold such a post – a year later she became the first female Fellow of the American Institute of Electrical Engineers.

The recipient of the Society of Women Engineers Achievement Award, she died in 1959.